Santa's Visit to Maryland

© Copyright 2023

No portion of this book may be reproduced, stored in a retrieval system or transmitted in any form or by any means—electronic, mechanical, photocopy, recording, scanning, or other—except for brief quotations and critical reviews or articles, without the prior written permission of the author, artist or publisher.

ISBN: 978-1-956581-29-4

Santa on sailboat image purchased from iStock and modified to look like watercolor.

Canyon Lake, Texas
www.ErinGoBraghPublishing.com

* Cover image redesigned by Kathleen's Graphics *

Listen to the Audio Book!

To really make this book come alive, select the musical background track composed especially for this reading.

Learn more at: www.facebook.com/santasvisit
Or Email the Author Directly: Santasvisit3@gmail.com

"Santa's visit to Maryland" captures what Santa might see as he flies over the state. Maryland is frequently viewed as "America in Miniature" with a sample of mountains, the bay and the ocean, sports, industry and tech. There is something for everyone!

Add some hot chocolate and a roaring fire so the whole family will be transported onto Santa's sleigh.

With hopes you'll consider this book an annual family Christmas tradition.

'Twas the night before Christmas and all through the bay
The creatures were waiting for Santa's new sleigh

The crab pots were hung by the dock with great care
Bright colored snowballs blew through the air

The children were nestled all snug in their beds, While dreams of Berger Cookies danced in their heads

Then out from the Chesapeake there arose such a splash,
The crabs and the oysters were havin' a bash.

The clams wanted cheer; they invited Natty Boh,
Edgar Allan Poe? No.... He didn't show.

More rapid than Route 50 his reindeer they came,
And he whistled and shouted and called them by name.

On Ripkin, on Tubman, Johns Hopkins, Under Armour,
Through Essex, Little It-ly, they were finally in "Baltimore"

His Reindeer dashed to the Maryland Zoo
And gave jingle bells to the caribou.

Saluting the flag at the Star-Spangled Banner
O'r Charm City they glided with glamour.

The Bay Bridge, Annapolis, he defied gravity, Air-dropping gifts to the Naval Academy.

The moon on the west of the Bromo Tower Gave luster to the city for over an hour.

Yet through all of this fun, Santa paused his activity
To kneel and give honor at a church's nativity.

Then off to the stadium, for his night on the town,
With the elves all chanting for a Ravens touchdown.

The reindeer hooves stomped a beat with applause,
As they cheered for the Ravens with Santa Claus.

Mrs. Claus dressed like a "Hampden Hon,"
Her hair in a beehive, and leopard skin on.

Then back to his business he hopped in his sleigh, expressing good wishes while soaring away.

To the west, Deep Creek and the east "downy ocean,"

Santa sprinkled good cheer with a festive potion

rough Gambrill's and Frederick, then on to Queen Anne,
He wrapped up his tour through Maryland.

And I heard him exclaim as he drove out of sight,
Ho Ho Ho from the Land of Pleasant Living,

MERRY CHRISTMAS and GOOD NIGHT!

Lynn Roxy Gambrill and Leo Kahl attended Perry Hall Senior High School together in Perry Hall, Maryland. Little did they know that years later they would compose a book together!

Lynn "Roxy" fronted the popular classic rock band, "The Fabulous Hubcaps" and covered lead vocals, keyboard, sax, and flute.

As a featured performer, she worked on cruise ships throughout the U.S. and Europe. Lynn played for over 20 years as the principal pianist with the 35-piece Trinity Symphony Orchestra. She continues to perform hundreds of gigs per year.

Lynn is the CEO of Roxy Piano Lessons. She is a jazz and classical faculty member at the Community Colleges of Baltimore County, and a member of the Maryland Entertainment Hall of Fame.

ERIN GO BRAGH Publishing

Erin Go Bragh Publishing publishes various genres of books for numerous authors. Their portfolio consists of a 1200-page Vietnamese to English Dictionary, Historical fiction, an award-winning children's educational series, multiple adult novels and memoires, tween adventure stories, poetry as well as Christian Fiction for all ages. Their objective is to promote literacy and education through reading and writing.

www.ErinGoBraghPublishing.com

Canyon Lake, Texas

www.ingramcontent.com/pod-product-compliance
Lightning Source LLC
Chambersburg PA
CBHW060824090426
42738CB00002B/96